Joseph Frederic Dripps

# Historical sketch of the missions in Siam and among the Laos

Joseph Frederic Dripps

**Historical sketch of the missions in Siam and among the Laos**

ISBN/EAN: 9783742892140

Manufactured in Europe, USA, Canada, Australia, Japa

Cover: Foto ©ninafisch / pixelio.de

Manufactured and distributed by brebook publishing software
(www.brebook.com)

Joseph Frederic Dripps

**Historical sketch of the missions in Siam and among the Laos**

# HISTORICAL SKETCH

OF THE

# Missions in Siam and among the Laos

UNDER THE CARE OF THE

## BOARD OF FOREIGN MISSIONS OF THE PRESBYTERIAN CHURCH.

## By REV. J. F. DRIPPS.

―――――――――

PUBLISHED BY THE
WOMAN'S FOREIGN MISSIONARY SOCIETY OF THE
PRESBYTERIAN CHURCH,
No. 1334 CHESTNUT STREET, PHILADELPHIA.

1881.

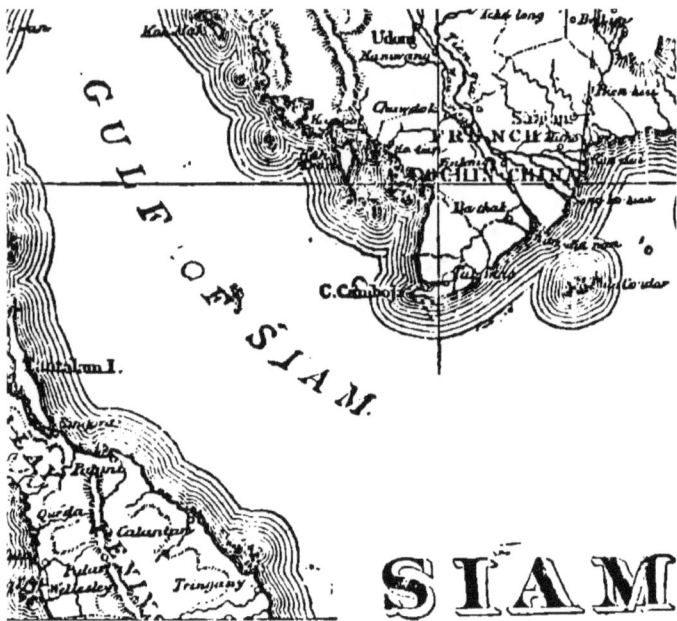

# MISSIONS IN SIAM.

CHINA on the extreme east, and India on the south—each has its definite place in our mind; but we cannot always say as much for the tract of land which lies between them, in the southeast corner of Asia, and known sometimes as Farther India or Indo-China. Siam occupies the central and larger portion of this corner-land, with Burmah on its west and Cochin China on the east, including also most of the long, narrow Malayan peninsula which juts out from the mainland and forms the sharply-defined corner of the continent. Beginning at the lower end of this peninsular portion, within five degrees of the equator, the Siamese territory extends 1350 miles to the north, and measures at its widest point some 450 miles from east to west. It contains 190,000 square miles, or about as much as New England with the four middle states.

Most of the country is a low-lying plain, completely overflowed every year by its four great rivers. Journeying northward along the chief river, this plain is found to continue for some four hundred miles, when great mountains close in upon the stream, and the traveller encounters more than forty very difficult rapids in the midst of singularly-impressive scenery; after which the country opens again into another wide plain, very much like the former one, and known as that of the Laos people. The annual overflow of the rivers, with the abundant rainfall, enables the production of such crops as rice and sugar in great abundance. It is claimed to be the garden-land of the world—the land of fruit and flowers and of never-ending summer, with grand old trees overshadowing every hamlet, and plant-life in fullest variety bursting on every side from the fertile soil.

It is also the land of elephants, the king having five thousand of them in his service for war purposes alone. One variety is that which is known to us as the "white" elephant, though the Siamese name for it is "the strange-colored," and it is really a whitish brown. Its form is used on the Siamese flags as the national symbol, and it is held in great honor, though not actually worshipped. There is great abundance of fish, as also of insects and, indeed, of every form of tropical life.

The climate of the whole country is genial and not unfavorable to health, though Europeans need to exchange it at intervals for

something more bracing, and the natives suffer considerably from malarial diseases. The thermometer varies from 64° to 99°, averaging 81°. There is a dry season from November to May, and a wet season for the other half of the year.

The population is but partly Siamese, nearly one-half being made up of the tributary races and of Chinese immigrants. There are perhaps five or six millions in all, though no exact statement has ever been given on this point. In any case, however, it is not a quarter of the number which the land could easily support, and the paucity is ascribed to such causes as war and disease, polygamy, and the celibacy of the priesthood. By descent the people are of the same family with the Chinese, having also several features of likeness to the natives of India. The name by which we call them is supposed to come from the Sanscrit word "*syam*," meaning "the brown," though they call themselves by a term signifying "the free." They are a gentle, passive, rather weak race, given to dissimulation, and very conceited; but they are reverential to the aged, especially to parents, are kind to their children, liberal in alms giving, orderly and peaceable. They have quick, though not very strong, minds, and are said to be more receptive than the Chinese. These traits are common to all the native races, though the Laos have a somewhat stronger character, with many interesting traits peculiar to itself. The universal inertness, due to the enervating climate, is confirmed by the fact that food is so excessively cheap, and that small exertion is required for satisfying the need of clothing, a waist-cloth having usually been all that was held necessary, with sometimes a light cape over the shoulders. A large proportion of the people have continued to live in a state which is nominally that of slavery, though it is of a mild type, and terminable at any time by the payment of a fixed sum. It is now in process of being entirely abolished, by order of the king. Women are not held in restriction, but go about the streets at will, and transact business freely. They are, however, considered to be of so inferior a nature that they are not educated at all, whereas most of the men and boys can read and write. Polygamy is usual among those who can afford it, and divorce is easy in all classes, though there are many happy marriages.

The government is an absolute monarchy, entrusting all power of every kind to the king. The "second king" has no share in the administration, nor have the nobles, although when the king dies it is the assembly of nobles which chooses his successor, either from among his sons or, if they prefer, from some other family.

The history of the country presents very little of importance or interest until the advent of Christian missionaries; since which time many features of western civilization have been adopted by

order of the present king and of his predecessor. In fact, the
change made in this direction has nothing to equal it, except in
the case of Japan.

Foreign commerce, with the encouragement which it is now
beginning to receive, is capable of immense expansion, so abundant
are the natural resources of every kind, and so readily accessible.
This feature of accessibility is especially marked. Not only can
the great rivers be readily made available, but the net-work of
canals which interlaces the country between them. This gives its
peculiar character to Bangkok, the capital, which has much the
same importance for Siam as London for England. This city, of
four hundred thousand inhabitants, situated not far from the sea,
has the chief river of the land for its main avenue and canals for
lesser ones. When the native houses are not built on piles driven
into the banks, they are often floated on platforms in the river
itself, whose sides are thus lined for several miles. The whole
city and, indeed, all lower Siam can be reached by boat—a fact
most important for commerce, as it is also for missionary work.

## BUDDHISM.

Considered as a field for Christian missions, the most noticeable
fact in regard to Siam is that it constitutes the very citadel of
Buddhism—the land which, more than any other, is entirely and
only Buddhist. In China, a Buddhist is also a Confucianist and a
Taoist; even his Buddhism itself being far less pure than in Siam.
This system attracts the more attention because within the present
generation it has become distinctly known by us for the first time.
The result is that while many still regard it as a mere tissue of
palpable absurdities, some of our writers are claiming for it a place
by the side of Christianity itself, and on a level with it.

The truth lies of course between such extremes. Buddhists
need Christianity as deeply as any men on earth; yet their own
system, with its strange mixture of good and evil, has a power
which is real and formidable. It is six hundred years older than
Christianity, having originated about the time of the Jewish
prophet Daniel, in an age which also witnessed the teaching of
Confucius among the Chinese, and of Pythagoras among the
Greeks; a time which was one of mental quickening and enlarge-
ment of thought over all the earth. Its founder himself was
commonly known by his family name Gautama, and by the title
of "The Buddha"—that is, "The Enlightened One." He has
left an impression, by his personal character and teachings, rarely
equalled among men. In Siam, for example, there has been for
twelve hundred years no other religion than his; one which is ven-
erated beyond expression, and interwoven with every act and occu-

pation of life. It has shown much of intellectual subtlety, and even of moral truth, mingled with all its absurdities and vices; and has proven itself singularly adapted to the people with whom it deals. Its influence is not only long-continued and deep, but very broad. It has greatly modified the other religions of India, though seven centuries ago it was finally driven from its place among them; while in China the whole population is enrolled among its adherents. One-half of mankind bear its impressions; one-third of them are its active supporters. It would be by all means the leading religion on earth if mere numbers could make it such.

Yet, in the real sense of the word, it is no religion at all, for it teaches no God above and no soul within us. Most of its followers have in their language no word whatever for that which we call "God," in the sense of a divine Ruler, Creator, Preserver of men, and the very idea of such a being does not exist in Buddhism. The Buddha himself was not a god, but a man; and though he speaks of beings who are called gods, yet they are described as mere mortals like ourselves, having no power over us, nor even any essential superiority to us. Each man must work out his own destiny for himself, with no aid from any higher power, in the spirit of atheistic rationalism.

Buddhism, as such, has therefore no such thing as prayer or religious worship in any form. The nearest approach to this is in the form of inward meditation, or of paying outward honors to the memory of Gautama by carrying flowers to his monument. When Buddhists wish to find any outlet for the religious instinct they must go outside of Buddhism to seek it. This is actually the case with nearly all of them. They crave some object of worship, and since Gautama has given them none, they addict themselves to some form of devil-worship or witchcraft by way of addition to his system. This single fact is sufficient commentary upon the fatal defectiveness of his teachings. They do also say prayers, which are in some cases the real cry of the soul toward some one or something which can help it. Usually, however, the "prayer" which they repeat is not so much in the form of appeal to any living hearer as in that of a charm or incantation; the mere repetition of the words being supposed to have magical power in itself. Hence originated the use of "praying-mills" in Thibet, each turn of the wheel being considered as a repetition of the prayer or magical form which is written upon it. In such ways as this Buddhism has come to receive an enormous mass of additions, many of which are directly opposed to its original teachings. A singular fact in this connection is the outgrowth of an extremely elaborate system of worship in Thibet, though not in Siam, which resembles closely in all its outward forms that of the Church of Rome. Even in Siam images

of Buddha are enormously multiplied, tending to practical idolatry. There are said to be fourteen thousand in one temple alone.

The atheism of Gautama's teaching is the more complete because of his declaring, in the most emphatic manner possible, that there is no such thing as soul or spirit in man himself; that a man is only a body with certain faculties added to it, all of which scatter into nothingness when the body dissolves. One feature of Buddhism, therefore, is its denial of all spirituality, divine or human.

A second feature is its assertion, as the positive facts upon which it builds, of two most remarkable ideas. One of these is the doctrine to which Gautama most frequently refers, and to which his followers have given most heed, viz., that of *transmigration*. This belief, strange as it seems to Christians, is held by most of the human race as affording the only explanation they can find for the perplexing inequalities of earthly experience. It teaches that the cause of every joy or sorrow is to be found in some conduct of the man himself, if not in this life, then in some of his previous lives. Such a theory appeals to the conviction that every event must have a cause, and to the innate sense of justice which demands that every act shall have its merited consequence. It also connects itself with that "strange trick of memory," as it has been called, which leads occasionally to the sudden sense of our having previously met the very scene, having said and done the very things which are now present with us; and as they say it cannot be disproved, its believers are slow to give it up. In fact, as the usual emblem of Christianity is the cross, so that of Buddhism is the wheel—chosen as such from its suggestion of endless rotation.

Buddhism, however, which denies the existence of the soul, is obliged to teach transmigration in a very strange form—a form, indeed, which is not only mysterious, but impossible. According to this, although you go to nothingness when you die, yet a new person is sure to be produced at that moment, who is considered to be practically the same as yourself, because he begins existence with all your merits and demerits exactly, and it is to your thirst for life that he owes his being. Yet, as it is acknowledged that you are not conscious of producing him and he is not conscious of any relation with you, it is hard to see how human brains can accept such a hopeless absurdity as this doctrine of "Karma." Practically, its believers are apt to forget their denial of the soul, and speak as if it does exist and goes at death into a new body. This new birth, moreover, may be not into the form of a man, but into that of a beast of the earth, a devil in some hell or an angel in some heaven. Buddhism not only teaches the existence of hells and heavens, but fixes their exact size and position; so that one glance through the telescope, or any acquaintance with

astronomy, is enough to prove the falsity of its declarations on that point. It is further taught that each of these future lives must come to an end, for all things above and below are continually changing places with each other, as they ever have done and ever will do. There is therefore no real satisfaction even in the prospect of a heavenly life, since it must in time change, probably for the worse, while the chief probability points to some new life which is worse, and not better, than the present.

In close connection, then, with this fundamental idea of Buddhism, namely transmigration, is the other idea that all life, present or future, is essentially so transitory, disappointing, and miserable, that the greatest of blessings would be the power to cease from the weary round entirely and forever. Practically its votaries have before their minds a life in some delightful heaven, which may be secured against turning into any following evil by passing instead into calm unending slumber. The essential features of this heavenly condition are its preception of life's illusiveness, with freedom from all resulting lusts and passions; and this ensures that when the life you are then living shall close, no new being will be formed in your place, because your thirst for living is at last extinguished. While it is true, then, that this condition of heavenly calm or *Nirvana* is represented as eminently attractive, yet its distinguishing benefit lies in the fact that when it ends, that which follows is not a new birth, but an eternal freedom from all life. This is in its essence a doctrine of despair, even though the annihilation of life is called by the softer name of endless slumber, and attention is mainly fixed on the joys of *Nirvana* which precede that slumber.

The remaining or third chief feature of Buddhism is its description of the "Noble Path"—the way by which a man is to reach this desired goal. Having (1) denied the existence of God and the soul, and (2) asserted the existence of transmigration and of an essential misery in all life, from which *Nirvana* is the only deliverance, it proceeds (3) to tell how *Nirvana* may be reached. It is by means of persevering meditation upon the hollowness of life, together with the practice of control over self and benevolence to others. Many of the rules given for this end have in them a moral truth and beauty which is exceedingly remarkable. The opposition made to caste and to extending religion by force of arms, the freedom given to woman, and the mildness of manners cherished among all, are most commendable. Much of its hold upon men undoubtedly came from the fact that its moral standard is endorsed to so great an extent by every man's conscience, while its spirit of self-help and of working out merit by one's own acts would find a responsive chord in most men. Gautama, the Buddha, must have been a noble man, far above the average around him in brain and heart,

and not the least so in his efforts to learn from others before beginning himself to teach. But his followers of to-day are by no means teachable in the presence of Christianity, with its fullness of divine truth; and whenever partial truth resists fuller truth it becomes wrong and hurtful. If Buddhism held faithfully the truth it knew, ever ready to learn further lessons of good, it could be viewed with gladness as a system which had prevented many a worse one, while not hindering aught better still; but this latter assertion cannot be made.

Its claim to be perfect and final is utterly wrong. On the one hand it absolutely ignores any thought of love and duty to God, or even the mention of His name, and even its benevolence to man arises from the desire of saving self. It has no living root, no true foundation. As the main thing is to save one's self from misery, separation from others is a cardinal virtue; the best form of life is that of the monk, and his goodness is most complete when he refuses even to look at a woman, or to have any share in healing the diseases of others. Such a theory is far removed from the benevolence of our Lord Jesus Christ. It commits also the natural mistake of forbidding a thing totally when it is only its excess which is evil, as where the man seeking perfection is forbidden to touch money at all or to take any life, etc. It must be remembered that disobedience to these moral laws is not called "sin," for where no God is recognized no sin is confessed, and it is merely so much loss to one's self, just as when any other law of nature is broken. If you choose to take the loss you are always at liberty to break the law. Morality becomes a mere affair of profit and loss; so that we even read of a Buddhist account-book, with its debtor and creditor columns, by which the yearly balance of merits or demerits could readily be ascertained.

We must beware then of putting Christian meaning into Buddhist words, or of supposing that such a description of Buddhism as Arnold's " Light of Asia," with all its poetic and spiritual beauties, could have been written by any man destitute of Christian ideas. Moreover, if there is fault and defect even in the purest possible form of the system, how much more is there in the actual teachings of Buddhist books after twenty-four hundred years of corruption.

The practical conduct of its followers is below even this faulty standard; they live as the heathen did whom Paul describes in the first chapter of his Epistle to the Romans. For after all, the great distinction between all other religions and Christianity is not merely that they present lower standards than it, but that they do not present at all that which is its one chief offer, viz., grace and strength whereby men become able to rise toward their standard. Buddhism makes no such offer as this, and has no conception of

1*

such a thing. It fixes the mind upon the evils and miseries of life, which it is by its own power to shun, and not upon the positive holiness and blessedness of a divine Father and Saviour, whose grace can lift the soul toward the glory which it sees.

Christians freely concede all that can truly be claimed for the Buddhist standard; for the higher it is, the more does it show natural conscience endorsing the requirements of God as no more than right and just. The defects of Buddhism, both in theory and practice, are evident enough. In all these twenty-four hundred years, and among these myriads of men, it has produced no single nation comparable with even the lowest of Christian states. In fact, the very existence of its priesthood, as seen in Siam, is enough to dwarf the prosperity of any people. The name of "priest" is, indeed, hardly accurate in this case, for the condition intended is rather that of a monk—of one who gives himself to carry into practice Gautama's conception of the best life. Each works out merit for himself by a life of meditation, without undertaking for others any work which is really "priestly." Forbidden to engage in useful work, and enjoined to live solely on alms, these men drain the community of $25,000,000 each year for their bodily support alone, beside all which they get for their temples, etc. This is at a rate which would amount, if Siam were as large as our own nation, to the enormous sum of $200,000,000 yearly for the personal support of priests. Ignorant as they usually are, yet the whole education of the people is in their hands; and every man in the nation spends at least part of his life in the priesthood, while every woman and child is glad to gain merit by feeding them. They not only control the nation, but may almost be said to include it, bodily; and it may be imagined how firmly they hold it to Buddhism. When it is possible for a man to say, as one of these priests did, "I do not worship the gods, but they worship me," and to really believe that by rigid perseverance in his system he can outrank any being in existence, it is evident that such pride will not readily confess itself wholly wrong, and accept any new religion.

How can a system be conceived more completely guarded against the entrance of Christianity, and at the same time more utterly in need of the gospel? It might readily be expected that missionary work would make slow progress under such circumstances. We can the better appreciate, then, that advance which has actually been made.

### ROMAN CATHOLIC MISSIONS.

The Church of Rome established its missions in Siam as early as 1662. The grand embassy from Louis XIV., a few years later, was accompanied by a number of priests, and from that time to the

present they have tenaciously held their ground, through periods of severe persecution or of contemptuous toleration, varied only occasionally by intervals of royal favor. They have found the work to be one of special difficulty, however, and their efforts have produced far less result than in most other missions conducted by them. Yet the size of their roll is still greater than that of the Protestant missions, and it is therefore necessary to remember that the difference in quality is so radical and complete that such a comparison of quantities is utterly misleading. This declaration would not be made if the Roman Church held the same standard in Siam which it does in England or America, instead of sinking, as it actually has done, almost to the level of heathenism itself. This can be tested by observing its attitude towards the "Christians," the Siamese, and the Chinese.

There is still quite a considerable body of mixed descendants from the early Portuguese settlers whom the Roman priests have succeeded in keeping from apostatizing to Buddhism; but their preservation as a distinct body bearing the name of "Christian" has been a very questionable benefit. Dr. Gutzlaff, for example, found that the servility and moral degradation of these "Christians" had inspired the Siamese with such contempt, not only for the religion but for the civilization and power of all Europeans, that they only began to change their minds upon finding that British arms had actually defeated and conquered Burmah, which is on the very border of Siam itself. What wonder is it that to such a body as this there have been added scarcely any converts whatever from among adult Siamese, and that the rolls of the Roman Church are enlarged mainly by claiming the names of those heathen infants who are surreptitiously baptized when at the point of death, by the priests or their assistants, under the guise of administering medicine?

From the Chinese traders Dr. House informs us that the Roman priests have received of late quite an accession, by offering as a consideration the protection of the French government, with consequent immunity from the many exactions and annoyances of the Siamese officials. It is very evident that a roll of names made up on such principles and for such a body can in no way be considered as a roll of Christian converts, and compared as such with that of Protestant churches. Whatever could be accomplished by Jesuit influence has always been tried, to induce the native government to expel from the country every gospel missionary. No retaliation for these attacks has been attempted, but it has been clearly perceived that the need of Siam for Protestant missions is not a particle the less, but rather the greater, because of the mission work of the Church of Rome.

## PROTESTANT MISSIONS.

"It is an interesting fact," says Dr. House, "that the very first effort made by any of the Protestant faith for the spiritual good of the people of Siam was by a woman. This was Ann Haseltine Judson, of sainted memory, who had become interested in some Siamese living at Rangoon, where she then resided. In a letter to a friend in the United States, dated April 30, 1818, she writes, 'Accompanying is a catechism in Siamese, which I have just copied for you. I have attended to the Siamese language for about a year and a half, and, with the assistance of my teacher, have translated the Burman catechism (just prepared by Dr. Judson), a tract containing an abstract of Christianity and the Gospel of Matthew, into that language.' The catechism was printed by the English Baptist mission press at Serampore in 1819, being the first Christian book ever printed in Siamese."

For more than twenty years after this time, however, Siam was regarded by mission workers chiefly as a point of approach to China, where nearly one-third of the human race were living in total ignorance of Christianity. It was in this way that Bangkok was visited in 1828 by the celebrated Dr. Karl Gutzlaff, whose works upon China are still of great value. He was then connected with the Netherland Missionary Society, and was accompanied by Rev. Mr. Tomlin, of the London society's mission at Singapore. They immediately gave their services as physicians to crowds of patients, and distributed twenty-five boxes of books and tracts in Chinese within two months. They connected with their Chinese work the study of Siamese, even attempting to translate the Scriptures into that language. Appeals were also sent by them to the American churches and the American Board of Commissioners for Foreign Missions, and to Dr. Judson in Burmah, urging that missionaries be sent to Siam. Mr. Tomlin was compelled by severe illness to return to Singapore in the following year. Late in 1829 Dr. Gutzlaff, having prepared a tract in Siamese and translated one of the Gospels, also visited Singapore to have them printed. While there he was married to Miss Maria Newell, of the London Missionary Society, the first woman to undertake personal work for Christ in Siam itself, whither she went a few months after their marriage. She lived, however, little more than a year after that time, and her babe soon followed her. Her husband, being extremely ill, was urged to sail northward to China itself, which, in spite of great peril, he succeeded in doing, and began, on his recovery, a singularly-adventurous pioneer work in that land. He was but twenty-five years of age when he reached Siam, and put forth all the energy of his nature into the work he found there.

The death of his devoted wife and his own enforced departure to China were felt to be no ordinary loss for Siam. A few days after he had sailed, in June, 1831, Rev. David Abeel arrived, having been sent by the American Board of Commissioners for Foreign Missions in answer to the appeal of Gutzlaff and Tomlin. Mr. Tomlin himself came with him, but could only remain for six months, when he was placed in charge of the Anglo-Chinese college at Malacca. After repeated experiments, Dr. Abeel also was compelled to give up work in Siam, on account of protracted ill-health, in November, 1832. The American Board thereupon sent out Rev. Messrs. Johnson and Robinson, who arrived in July, 1834, and D. B. Bradley, M.D., in July, 1835. "Like all their predecessors, these missionaries had some knowledge of the healing art and a stock of medicines for free distribution; so that the people of Siam naturally give to every Protestant missionary the title of 'mau,' or 'doctor of medicine.'" Several of them have been fully-trained physicians, among whom was Dr. Bradley. "His work as medical missionary, writer and translator into Siamese of Christian books, printer, and preacher, continued with a zeal and hope which knew neither weariness nor discouragement until his lamented death, after thirty-eight years of toil, in June, 1873." Two of his daughters, Mrs. McGilvary and Mrs. Cheek, still continue on the field as the wives of Presbyterian missionaries. Upon the opening of China to missionary work, the American Board transferred its efforts to that country, and gave its field in Siam to the "American Missionary Society," by which the work was maintained for some years longer, and then discontinued.

An American Baptist mission to the Chinese in Siam is still carried on with great success by the veteran soldier of the cross, Rev. Dr. Dean, who was its founder in 1835. There was for many years another department of the mission, beginning still earlier, in 1833, and addressing itself to the Siamese themselves. This has now for several years been discontinued, and the entire strength of the Baptist mission is concentrated upon its work for the Chinese, which proved to be much the more successful of the two. These Chinese, it will be understood, keep themselves as distinct from the natives as they do in our own land. They are much the more energetic race, and have rapidly accumulated for themselves the positions of profitable enterprise in the land. If the Siamese are permanently to hold their own, they greatly need the stimulating influence of Christian religion and civilization. They have traits of their own, however, which are peculiarly favorable to such development, and we have cause, not only for the sense of responsibility but for hopeful effort, in the fact that the entire work of Christianizing the natives of Siam is left to the Presbyterian Church.

Ours is the only Siamese mission which has remained in permanent operation.

## PRESBYTERIAN MISSIONS.

The first visit made to Siam by any representative of our own Church was for the same purpose which had already brought other missionaries there—namely, to find some door of access to the Chinese. This was in November, 1838, when Rev. Mr. Orr spent a month in Bangkok, and thereupon recommended our Board of Foreign Missions to take this country as a field of effort, not only for the Chinese, but for the Siamese themselves. In accordance with this recommendation the Rev. W. P. Buell was sent to Bangkok, where he arrived in 1840. After remaining until 1844 and doing good foundation work, he was compelled to leave the field to bring home Mrs. Buell, who had been stricken with paralysis. Arrangements were made to fill his place as soon as possible, but from various reasons it was not until 1847 that the next missionaries actually reached Siam. From that time until the present, continuous work has been maintained; and as the Chinese could then be reached in their own land, our mission here addressed itself directly to the native Siamese.

The Rev. Stephen Mattoon and wife, with Rev. S. R. House, M.D., were the missionaries who began work in that year. Their foothold seemed, however, very precarious for several years afterward, on account of the active, though secret, opposition of the king. Without openly using force, he so exerted his despotic influence upon the slavish people that none of them could be induced to rent or sell any house to the missionaries, and a most effectual obstacle to their work was thus presented. Other difficulties of the same general nature were put in their way, and it seemed quite certain that they would actually be edged away from the land altogether.

About the same time Sir James Brooks, who had arrived to open negotiations with the king on behalf of the British government, found himself treated in a manner which he considered so insulting that he indignantly took ship again with the purpose of securing assistance in the effort to open the country by main force. Just at the moment when all these complications were at their height, the death of the king was announced (April 3, 1851). This event brought about a complete change in the whole situation, and in all the succeeding history of the country; a change which is directly traceable to the influence of Protestant missions. The man whom the assembly of nobles elected to fill the throne, and who reigned from 1851 until the end of 1868, proved to be very liberal in all his policy. When the next embassy from the British

government reached Siam, under Sir John Bowring, it was to find on the throne no longer an ignorant, unmanageable barbarian, but a man who could appreciate civilization, and who claimed to be himself quite a scholar even by European standards. This came from the fact that while still in private life he was occupied much of his time, under the instruction of a Baptist missionary, in the study of language and of modern science.

For the thirty years which have now intervened since his accession, Protestant missionaries have been accorded very noticeable influence with the government. In estimating the result of their work, this fact must be given much prominence. An official document, under the royal sanction, makes the following statement: " Many years ago the American missionaries came here. They came before any other Europeans, and they taught the Siamese to speak and read the English language. The American missionaries have always been just and upright men. They have never meddled in the affairs of government, nor created any difficulty with the Siamese. They have lived with the Siamese just as if they belonged to the nation. The government of Siam has great love and respect for them, and has no fear whatever concerning them. When there has been a difficulty of any kind, the missionaries have many times rendered valuable assistance. For this reason the Siamese have loved and respected them for a long time. The Americans have also taught the Siamese many things."

Reference is also frequently made to the statement of a regent that " Siam was not opened by British gunpowder like China, but by the influence of missionaries." No estimate of mission work would be complete, therefore, which did not include its connection with these great changes in the whole attitude and condition of the nation, which have already astonished the world, and which are of still ampler promise for the future. Though such results may be considered as indirect and preparatory, they are to be thankfully acknowledged before God, who has chosen to attest His blessing and help in this form, while not omitting further tokens of a more immediately spiritual nature.

Perhaps the best way to view the course of our work will be to look at it in connection with the places which have successively been taken up as centres of effort, among both Siamese and Laos.

## BANGKOK.

The first convert in connection with the mission was the Chinese teacher Qua-Kieng, who was baptized in 1844, and died in the faith in 1859. It is interesting to learn that three of his children became Christians after his death, one of them a candidate for the ministry. This is by no means the only instance in the history of

the mission in which the baptized children, either of foreign or of native laborers, have taken up the work of their fathers.

A good record is also given of Nai Chune, the first native Siamese convert. "Though frequently offered positions of honor, lucrative offices and employment by the government, he refuses all and chooses to support himself by the practice of medicine, that thus he may the more readily carry the gospel message."

It was not until 1859, however, that this first convert was made. Twelve long years had elapsed before the missionaries of 1847 were given the joy of gathering any first-fruits of their labors. Such a period of delay has not been unknown in the history of several other mission fields, which became thereafter eminently successful, and in view of all the obstacles in the case now before us, it can hardly be thought surprising. Instead of causing His servants to reap immediately, by bringing one part of the field into full maturity, the Master chose, as we have seen, to use them for doing long-continued preparatory work, which will in the end attest His wisdom as the Lord of the harvest. Tokens have moreover come to light within recent years which show that there really was success, even of a directly spiritual nature, where there were no signs visible to the workers through the years of patient perseverance. For example, several years after Dr. Bradley's death a marked instance of conversion was found, which was traceable directly to his faithful efforts in the printing and distribution of Christian truth. In a letter from the Laos mission in May, 1878, we are told of a visit made some months earlier, in June, 1877, by a venerable stranger, evidently a man of high rank, who came to ask medicine for his deafness, and referred to the miraculous cure which Christ had wrought upon a deaf man. He proved to be the highest officer of the court in the province of Lakaron, and at the time of this visit was seventy-three years of age. Twenty years before, he had visited Bangkok and received religious books from Dr. Bradley. They were printed in the Siamese character, which is so different from that used by the Laos, though the languages themselves are much the same, that he could not at the time read them, but learned the Siamese character for the purpose of so doing. He gave inward assent to the truth contained in them so far as he could understand it, but had never found any missionary to give him further instruction in his far-off home. He was now brought, for further light, to a place where meantime a Christian mission had been established for his nation. The path was opened by Divine Providence in his case, as in that of so many others in every age and land, through God's overruling of human persecution. His firmness of principle now brought upon him such trouble in his own province that he had

come to Chieng-mai, where he immediately sought out the missionaries. From that time he made this matter his one study, obtaining Buddhist books from the temple, and comparing them with Christian books, in the full exercise of that keen, practical sagacity for which he was noted. He intended to present himself at the communion-table in April, but was obliged to remain at home under a severe attack of illness. At the next communion, however, he made his appearance, declaring his conviction that the healing of his disease had been in answer to prayer. The missionary who moderated the session at his examination had seldom heard a more satisfactory and intelligent confession of faith in Christ than was given by him. As soon as he was known to be a Christian he was ordered back to his native city far away. His death was not unlikely to be the result; but he said to his Christian friends, "If they want to kill me because I worship Christ, and not demons, I will let them pierce me." His life was spared in the end, but office, wealth, and social position were taken, and he was ignored by all his friends. Later still we hear of him as starting to walk all the way to Chieng-mai, being too impoverished to command any mode of conveyance more suitable for his old age. His object in coming was to hear still further about the Lord Jesus, and the result of this second visit was the return with him of two native members from the Chieng-mai church to begin work in his native city. Out of this there is now developing one of our most promising out-stations; and the whole affair is traceable directly to the patient work of that early missionary, who never in this life came to know anything of it.

Another instance of the same kind is mentioned in a letter of Rev. Mr. Dunlap from Petchaburi in February, 1879. He speaks of visiting a very old Christian, who was evidently near his end, and there learning that he had received portions of the Bible from Dr. Bradley many years before, which he had hidden for fear of the authorities, and studied in secret, until he accepted Christ as there revealed, and put away his idols. Since that time his life had been that of a devoted Christian, active in work for other souls. Near him in his sickness lay his Bible and other books, among them the "Pilgrim's Progress," which he said he had read and re-read with joy. "The aged disciple," writes Mr. Dunlap, "said to the native preacher who accompanied me, 'I pray every day, but often wonder if I pray aright; if you will listen I will tell you, that you may teach me.' I listened also, and to such a prayer! It was full of humility, faith, and thanksgiving. He had plainly been taught by the best and highest of teachers."

No doubt these cases are but specimens of a class in which spiritual results were really gained during the very years which

seemed so barren of immediate fruit. Since the time when the first open confession was made by a native convert, other members have been steadily gathered into the churches, and the work, though it may be considered as still very largely in its preparatory stage, has many a token of encouraging success. All the usual forms of Christian effort are employed with diligence and effectiveness.

*Preaching*, both in chapels and by the wayside, has been given from the very beginning that prominence which justly belongs to it as the ordinance of Christ for the saving of souls. Whatever else is done, this is also done. The establishment of stations for regular preaching, and the organization of churches, have received full attention wherever God opened the way.

*The Press* affords another agency of especial importance among a people where four-fifths of the men and boys are able to read. The mission press at Bangkok is constantly sending forth copies of the Scriptures in Siamese, with translations from such books as the "Pilgrim's Progress," the "Child's Book of the Soul," etc., and also tracts and books prepared especially for this purpose. Its publication of the Siamese Hymnal has also proved very serviceable among a music-loving race. It may be mentioned that the Bible itself is usually printed in separate portions only, on account of the fact that a complete copy, even in the smallest Siamese type, would make a volume of larger size than our Webster's Unabridged Dictionary. In April, 1881, the whole Bible had been translated, except the books of Chronicles, which were in progress; and most of it had been printed. The delay in translating is caused by the need of accuracy, such as can only be ensured by employing men who have been long on the field and have become very familiar with the language. There have been in use, almost from the very beginning, translations of the Gospels and of some other books which have served a good purpose for the time; but the preparation of a standard Siamese Bible, which is greatly needed, is of much slower and more difficult attainment. The language is one which does not lend itself to the expression of truths so elevated as those of Scripture, with as much facility as some others which appear less promising. In 1880 there were printed 2500 copies of Matthew and 1000 each of five Old Testament books, besides much other matter.

*Medical work* has also been a most valuable adjunct of missionary effort, and this in two ways. Here, as in every land, it opens a way to the hearts of men by its self-denying beneficence, and affords many an opportunity of pointing the sin-sick soul to the Great Physician. But there is also the further effect of undermining the native confidence in the efficacy of spirit-worship. The mere fact of finding malaria healed through the use of quinine by one

of the native assistants is mentioned as producing a marked impression of this kind. It helps to convince them that Christianity shows itself to be of God by its harmony with all other truth, even in nature and science; whereas the whole teachings of Buddhism regarding its system of heavens and hells are contradicted and disproved by the science of astronomy, and the employment of incantations and witchcraft for the sick is proven to be false and useless by the scientific medical practice introduced by missionaries. The opportunities for such service are abundant. Thirty-four years ago Dr. House found this at the very beginning of his practice to such an extent that in the first eighteen months he treated 3117 patients. The need of such practice was shown in a terrible way soon afterward, when cholera was carrying off its victims at the rate of 30,000 a month. So favorable is the impression produced upon the Siamese by this work that they are now taking it up for themselves. In 1881 it is noted that a hospital for 60 patients had been erected and given for public use by a native nobleman, and in charge of native attendants; the physician in charge being Dr. Tien Hee, who had graduated some years earlier from the missionary boarding-school at Bangkok, and afterward from the Medical School of the University of the City of New York. The very existence and operation of such a hospital is a living argument against Buddhism, of unceasing and ever-widening operation. The sad need of it, even for the purpose of humane care for the suffering, was shown immediately after its erection, during the renewed visitation of cholera in the summer of 1881, when the death-rate in Bangkok had risen to five hundred a day at the very beginning of July. Surely there is abundant material for prayer to the Great Physician at our missionary concerts, in view of such facts as these. The devoted efforts of Christian physicians, laboring in the midst of all dangers, and, in such cases as that of the veteran Dr. House, for the period of a whole generation, deserve the most cordial recognition and support.

*Education* has, of course, a most important bearing upon mission work. The experience of Dr. Duff in India, and in fact that of all who have fairly tried the experiment, confirm everything which has been already said of the benefit secured by showing the heathen that scientific facts are never contradictory to the real doctrine of the Christian Scriptures, while such facts are always contradictory to the systems of false religion. Even the ordinary lessons of the day-school are found to produce among heathen families a powerful impression concerning religion, while of course the missionary teachers embrace every suitable opportunity for directly religious effort. There was at first no small difficulty in persuading any of the Siamese to come and be taught, and even in securing a really

desirable site for a school. The premises first occupied for the mission at Bangkok, and the best which could at the time be obtained, were at the lower end of the city. Here are two dwelling-houses, a chapel and room for the printing press, together with the school-house for boys. It was years after this before another lot was procured, some five miles further up the river in an excellent position, opposite some of the palaces and amidst the better residences. Here is a house for the missionaries and one for the girls' boarding-school.

The boys' school began work as early as 1852, and had an attendance in 1880 of sixty-seven; the girls' school, organized much later, had thirty attendants at the same date. There is an organized church at each of these points made up in part of the membership of the schools.

Great encouragement has been felt because of the interest and approbation manifested by the government in all our educational work. The recent appointment by the king of Dr. MacFarland to be principal of the Royal College at Bangkok and Superintendent of Public Instruction at large is very noteworthy. The large salary given for this service enables Dr. MacFarland to dispense with any support from the Board of Foreign Missions, while he still continues voluntarily to preach and teach Christianity in addition to the important work of his new position, whose influence is of incalculable advantage to the whole cause.

## PETCHABURI.

This city, one hundred miles southwest of the capital, is the favorite sanitary resort for Europeans and for the court. Though numbering but twenty thousand inhabitants, it is the central point of influence for a district containing a population of five hundred thousand. It is a significant fact that when Petchaburi was visited by a missionary in 1843 his books were refused, and every attempt to exert even a passing influence for Christianity was repulsed in the most uncompromising manner by the authorities. In 1861, however, it was by the urgent request of the governor that a station was formed at this point. Two years later there were three native converts applying for membership, and a church was thereupon organized, which has been steadily growing ever since.

School work is very prominent in Petchaburi. There were eight schools at different points in the city in 1880, and the Girls' Industrial School has much of special interest connected with it. In 1865, when the ladies tried to induce some of the ignorant half-grown girls of the neighborhood to come and be taught sewing, with reading and writing, there was much difficulty in securing even one. The idea of teaching a girl anything was so com-

pletely novel that the greatest opposition was made by the parents, as well as the girls themselves, to such an undertaking. The results in this case, however, approved themselves so well that the new enterprise grew in favor, and before very long the two ladies had forty-five girls in their charge, which was quite as many as they could care for, with all their other activities. In 1880 there were forty-nine in attendance. Soon after this was begun an invitation was extended to younger scholars, for whom a primary school was formed. In this case also the result was most encouraging. Parents would come to visit the school, repeating there the Scripture verses which they had caught from their children.

At one of the other schools the two native teachers were Christians, and the report also mentions that all but two of the thirty-eight scholars were from families in which were some church members; so that they were to some extent becoming surrounded by Christian influences. "The girls," we are told, "learn to make clothes and wear them, to find it possible to live without swearing or chewing betel." The filthy practice of chewing a mixture of tobacco and the betel nut, which is universal, and that of being what we should call half-naked, which is slowly being corrected, would be very sure to attract the attention of any Christian woman. The details of daily work in these schools are full of interest, and it is greatly to be desired that the *Foreign Missionary* magazine and the *Woman's Work for Woman*, which record many such facts, should have a largely-increased body of regular readers. In the present sketch it is only possible to indicate in passing that which can be found in those magazines with full details. The interest of the Siamese is shown by the fact that the king gave $1000, and his nobles $1300 more, for the new school building.

*The native ministry* began to receive its development at this station. In 1866 the license to preach was for the first time given to a native Christian, and there were four licentiates at work in the mission in 1880. The native preacher who is mentioned in a letter from Petchaburi, dated 1880, bears the marks of an excellent Christian. He was so affectionately attached to the elder of his church that the death of the latter brought upon him a severe illness, which threatened his own life. He is depicted as faithful in family training, constant in preaching labors, in acting as assistant surgeon also, vaccinating the people, and giving help of any kind wherever needed. Emergencies requiring just such ready helpers are not seldom found, as, for example, in the cholera scourge of 1881, which was fearfully prevalent not only in Bangkok, but throughout many other cities. The letter of Miss Cort, in the *Foreign Missionary* of October, 1881, presents a picture of desperate suffering all around, and of pure Christian devotedness,

which is intense in its very simplicity.  It is greatly to be depre-
cated that such a station should be left, as Petchaburi was in 1880,
for several months without any ordained minister on the ground.
The ladies of the mission cared faithfully for its interests, but
there are many needful services which in a heathen city cannot be
performed by ladies.  It looks as if they really needed to be helped
in their own work, and not to be taken off from it to do a service
which calls urgently for new recruits.  The missionary work done
by these Christian women on their journeys through the country
gives further token of their earnestness and tact.  Fresh life and
courageous effort may be seen on every side, indeed, in the oper-
ations of this little Christian band as a whole.

### OUT-STATIONS.

The best sign of health in any church, in the foreign field or at
home, is the existence of an aggressive spirit, leading the members
to go out to the world around them with their prayers, gifts, and
efforts.  This sign marks both of the churches at which we have
been looking.

From Bangkok mission effort extended itself to the city of
Ayuthia, some distance further up the river.  This point was
occupied as a regular station in 1872, and since the departure of
Rev. Mr. Carrington, in 1875, it has been carried on by native
effort.  The two churches of Bangkok combined in the erection of
a chapel and house, as well as the support of a native teacher.

The Petchaburi mission has stations at Bangk-boon and Waug-
tako, each with its chapel for regular preaching, and there are
also other points of effort which mark this as a field of much
promise.

### THE LAOS MISSION.

This name indicates an organization which is distinct and separate, though it is grouped with the Siamese mission in our reports,
and is of course very closely connected with it.  The Laos people,
it will be remembered, are distinct from the Siamese, though sub-
ject to the royal government.  The upper plain which has already
been described as their home, though but five hundred miles above
Bangkok, is practically further from it than is New York itself, if
the distance is estimated by the length of time required for the
journey.  The rapids in the river and the almost impassable mountains on each side of it present a barrier not quickly passed over.
Chieng-mai, the capital, was visited by a deputation from the Siam
mission in 1863, and in 1867 and 1868 Messrs. McGilvary and
Wilson came to remain.  They were soon encouraged by the con-

version of Nan Inta, a man who had thoroughly studied Buddhism and was dissatisfied with it, while knowing of nothing to replace it. He was much impressed by having the eclipse of August 18, 1868, foretold by the missionary a week in advance. He found the science of the Christians disproving the fables of Buddhism, and at once began eagerly to study the more directly spiritual truths connected with Christianity. He was soon able to make an intelligent confession of faith in Christ, and seven other converts were baptized within a few months. At this point the infant church was brought to a season of persecution and martyrdom. The king of the Laos, who usually exercised full control over his own people, though tributary to Siam, began to manifest the hostility which he had thus far concealed. Noi Soonya and Nan Chai were arrested, and on being brought before the authorities confessed that they had forsaken Buddhism. The "death-yoke" was then put around their necks, and a small rope was passed through the holes in their ears (used for ear-rings by all the natives), and carried over the beam of the house, to which they were thus tied as tightly as they could bear it. After being thus tortured all night they were again examined in the morning, but steadfastly refused to deny their Lord and Saviour even in the face of death. They prepared for execution by praying unto Him, closing with the words, "Lord Jesus, receive my spirit." Being then taken off to the jungle they were clubbed to death by the executioner, and one of them, not dying quickly enough, was thrust through the heart by a spear. The whole record is like one from the apostolic age, and speaks vividly of the first martyrs and of the same Lord by whose living presence they were sustained. Such fruits of the Spirit are unmistakable.

The persecution which thus began checked seriously for the time any progress in mission work. Shortly after this, however, the king died, and progress was resumed. Several new converts were soon received, and it was found that these cases of martyrdom had produced a deep impression for good. Still later, in 1878, another crisis was encountered, though less serious in its nature. The missionaries had decided to perform the marriage ceremony between two native Christians who had applied to them, and to do this without making any provision for the customary feast to the demons. The relatives, who were all devil-worshippers, prevented the marriage on this account, and the authorities supported them in the refusal. An appeal was at once made to the king of Siam, which brought for reply a "Proclamation of Religious Liberty to the Laos," which has placed the whole matter on a new basis and entirely changed the conduct of the officials. This proclamation was viewed as a great step in advance. It will be seen that

although Buddhism is theoretically opposed both to persecution and to devil-worship, yet Buddhists can be practically guilty of both the one and the other.

The pulpit and the press, the school-house and the hospital, are to be given active operation here, as in the Siamese mission.

The work of printing has been delayed by the great difficulty in procuring suitable type. The characters used, as noted above, are entirely different from those employed by the Siamese; and the diversified nature of a missionary's work would be vividly realized by any one who should read Mr. Wilson's experience with the type foundries in New York and Boston, followed by other difficulties on the field. The work of translating and printing is urged forward with all diligence.

Dr. Check's temporary hospital, though but a mere shed of bamboo, is described as rendering most important service to the whole cause, and well deserving to be replaced with a permanent building.

The girls' boarding-school is most successfully managed, and one for boys is in course of establishment. This department of the work met with sad bereavement in February, 1881, by the drowning of Miss Mary Campbell on her way back from a visit to Bangkok. The narrative as given by Miss Hartwell, in the *Foreign Missionary* for May, 1881, is full of pathetic interest. Dr. Check's watchful care to prevent any accident, and his persistent efforts at rescue, even when himself so nearly drowned as to be deprived of the power of speech, are fully recognized; as is also the fatal superstition which kept the natives from rendering any assistance, and the power of Christian principle in the native girl who alone of them all had just shaken off the fear of demons, and plunged into the water to do what she could. There is an urgent call for reinforcements, not only to fill up the gaps, but to increase the aggressive work. In every direction there is an open door inviting entrance.

The *Chieng-mai church* is growing well, both in numbers and in grace. One of the good signs is in the fact that a prayer-meeting is conducted each week by native elders and church members, with careful preparation and evident usefulness.

The *Bethlehem church* was organized in July, 1880, at a point some nine miles from Chieng-mai. This was the result of an interesting awakening of inquiry among the natives, who had heard of Christianity from relatives visiting the capital.

The *Lakouw church* has also been organized, at a distance of ninety miles from the parent congregation. One of the Chieng-mai members, having his residence at this point, had instructed a little band in Christian truth, so that they were ready for baptism when the missionary should visit them.

*Rahang*, on the frontiers of Siam, half way between Chieng-mai and Bangkok, is described as inviting regular occupancy. During Mr. McGilvary's visit, in 1880, he met several inquirers and applicants for baptism. Two were actually baptized, and one received instruction as a candidate for the ministry.

## THE OUTLOOK.

In both of the missions at which we have now glanced, the prospect is decidedly encouraging. It is true that in point of actual members it has only been since 1860 that any visible results appeared, and the roll (at the beginning of 1881) included but three hundred and fourteen names. The rate of progress, however, since the advance did begin has steadily increased, so that in one year the Siamese churches were increased by one-quarter and those of the Laos by nearly one-half of their previous number.

There are other tokens, moreover, less easily stated in figures, but no less obvious. Buddhism is shown to be losing ground by such facts as these: fewer men go into the priesthood, so that in Bangkok there are but half as many as there were some years since. "Monasteries which formerly had from seventy-five to one hundred priests have now not over twenty." Those who do enter the priesthood remain for a shorter term than formerly. "The king himself only remained in the priesthood a month, and his younger brother recently entered it for three days." Our inference from such a fact is confirmed by the further statement that the leading priests are themselves becoming so alarmed that they are taking vigorous measures to defend Buddhism by printing and distributing books which attack Christianity and uphold the native religion. We are reminded of the fact that when the early missionaries arrived in Siam a native nobleman said to them, "Do you with your little chisel expect to remove this great mountain?" Years afterward, when one of those missionary pioneers had died, though without seeing any fruit of his labors, another nobleman exclaimed, "Dr. Bradley is gone, but he has undermined Buddhism in Siam." It was a felicitous expression. "Undermining" is a form of work in which every stroke tells with the greatest advantage. Even a chisel may be used with success against a massive cliff if it be employed to "undermine" it. The missionaries have cut their little channels under the cliff, and laid up here and there the magazines of spiritual power, in full expectation that the electric flash of divine fire would in due time pass through the channels, and split in pieces the mighty rock.

But it is not enough to do merely this negative work. There is pressing need of positively Christianizing the land as it becomes emptied of Buddhism, else the last state of this people will be

worse than the first. Infidelity is no improvement upon even Buddhism. Our chief encouragement is in the evident presence of that living Lord who can bless the more positive work of building up Christianity, as He has blessed the negative work of undermining Buddhism. The men who occupy the outposts on the field itself regard themselves as anything but a "forlorn hope," while their weapons are proving "mighty through God to the casting down of strongholds." We, who read of it all from afar, can surely do our part in standing by them with prayer and sympathy and every needful support. The "Captain of the host of the Lord" may well look to us also for that "obedience of faith" which shows itself by trusting in Him as to the wisdom of the plan and the certainty of its success, while meantime we simply obey our standing orders by doing all we can to "preach the gospel to every creature."

●

## MISSIONARIES, 1881.

### SIAM.

BANGKOK.—Rev. Messrs. Noah A. McDonald and James W. Van Dyke and their wives; Miss Mary E. Hartwell, Miss Hattie H. McDonald, and Miss Laura A. Olmstead.

PETCHABURI.—Rev. C. S. McClelland and E. A. Sturge, M.D., and their wives; Miss Sarah Coffman and Miss Mary L. Cort.

### AMONG THE LAOS.

CHIENG-MAI.—Rev. Messrs. Daniel McGilvary, D.D., and Jonathan Wilson and their wives; Milton A. Cheek, M.D., and his wife; Miss Edna S. Cole and Miss S. Archibald.

---

### BOOKS OF REFERENCE.

The Land of the White Elephant. F. Vincent. $3.50.

Siam; or, the Land of the White Elephant. Rev. Mr. Bacon. $1.50.

Siam: its Government, Manners, and Customs. Rev. N. A. McDonald. $1.25.

The Journal of Dr. Abeel.

Manual of Buddhism. Rev. R. Spence Hardy.

Buddhism. T. W. Rhys Davids. 75 cents.

Fan-Kwei. Dr. W. M. Wood, U. S. N. $1.50.

# Missionaries in Siam and Laos, 1840–1881.

* Died. Figures, Term of Service in the field.

| | | | |
|---|---|---|---|
| Anderson, Miss A., | 1872–1876 | Hartwell, Miss M. E., | 1879– |
| Archibald, Miss S., | 1881– | House, Rev. S. R. (M.D.), | 1847–1876 |
| Arthur, Rev. R., | 1871–1873 | House, Mrs. H. N., | 1856–1876 |
| Arthur, Mrs., | 1871–1873 | McCauley, Rev. J. M., | 1875–1880 |
| *Buell, Rev. William P., | 1840–1844 | McCauley, Mrs. (Miss J. | |
| Buell, Mrs., | 1840–1844 | Kooser), | 1878–1880 |
| Bush, Rev. Stephen, | 1849–1853 | McClelland, Rev. C. S., | 1880– |
| *Bush, Mrs., | 1849–1851 | McClelland, Mrs., | 1880– |
| Carden, Rev. Patrick I.., | 1866–1869 | McDonald, Rev. Noah A., | 1860– |
| Carden, Mrs., | 1866–1869 | McDonald, Mrs., | 1860– |
| Carrington, Rev. John, | 1869–1875 | McDonald, Miss H. H., | 1879– |
| Carrington, Mrs., | 1869–1875 | McFarland, Rev. S. G., | 1860–1878 |
| Coffman, Miss S., | 1874– | McFarland, Mrs., | 1860–1878 |
| Cort, Miss M. I.., | 1874– | Mattoon, Rev. S., | 1847–1866 |
| Culbertson, Rev. J. N., | 1871–1881 | Mattoon, Mrs., | 1847–1866 |
| Culbertson, Mrs. (Miss B. | | Morse, Rev. Andrew B., | 1856–1858 |
| Caldwell), | 1878–1881 | Morse, Mrs., | 1856–1858 |
| Dickey, Miss E. S., | 1871–1873 | *Odell, Mrs. John F., | 1863–1864 |
| Dunlap, Rev. E. P., | 1875–1880 | Olmstead, Miss L. A., | 1880– |
| Dunlap, Mrs., | 1875–1880 | Sturge, E. A. (M.D.), | 1880– |
| George, Rev. S. C., | 1862–1873 | Sturge, Mrs., | 1881– |
| George, Mrs., | 1862–1873 | Van Dyke, Rev. James W., | 1869– |
| Grimstead, Miss S. D., | 1874–1877 | Van Dyke, Mrs., | 1869– |

## LAOS.

| | | | |
|---|---|---|---|
| *Campbell, Miss M. M., | 1879–1881 | McGilvary, Mrs., | 1860– |
| Cheek, M. A. (M.D.), | 1875– | *Vrooman, C. W. (M.D.), | 1871–1873 |
| Cheek, Mrs., | 1875– | Wilson, Rev. Jonathan, | 1858– |
| Cole, Miss E. S., | 1879– | *Wilson, Mrs. Maria, | 1858–1860 |
| McGilvary, Rev. D., | 1858– | Wilson, Mrs., | 1866– |

Compiled from lists prepared by Rev. J. C. Lowrie, D.D., Secretary of the Presbyterian Board of Foreign Missions.